The Shakespeare Quiz & Puzzle Book

by
Maggie Lane

Abson Books   Abson   Wick   Bristol

To Rupert

ABSON BOOKS, Abson, Wick, Bristol, England
First published in Great Britain, November 1984.

© Maggie Lane
Design: Paul Lane.
Typesetting: Gina Shepperd

All Rights Reserved. No part of this publication may be reproduced, stored in a retrieval system, or transmitted in any form by any means, electronic, mechanical, photocopying, recording or otherwise, without the prior permission of the publishers, with the exception of the teaching profession for use in schools.

ISBN 0 902920 56 1
Printed at the Burleigh Press Ltd. Bristol, England.

Introduction

Inspired by the plays of William Shakespeare, the quizzes and puzzles in this little book are designed to test your knowledge, exercise your skill, and perhaps refresh your memory.

The format follows that which has been well received in my other literary quiz and puzzle books. Each **crossword** is based upon an individual play, the clues consisting entirely of quotations from it. Some of the **quizzes** too are composed of quotations with a missing word, whilst others pose direct questions on a variety of topics touched on in the plays.

To solve the **name games,** each of which is devised from the **dramatic personae** of a particular play, fit the names of the principal characters into the squares reading across, and between the bold vertical lines a further character's name will appear.

Heroes, Heroines, Place Names, and Fools and Fairies are the subjects of the four **word search** puzzles. Hidden in the grid of letters are names from the appropriate category. The words may read backwards or forwards, horizontally, vertically or diagonally, and letters may be used more than once or not at all. Encircle the words on the grid as you find them, ticking them off the list as you go.

It was Jane Austen who made one of her characters say, "Shakespeare one gets acquainted with without knowing how. It is part of every Englishman's constitution. His thoughts and beauties are so spread abroad that one touches them everywhere, one is intimate with him by instinct". In compiling this book I have concentrated on the passages we are all familiar with, in the belief that it is always a pleasure to come upon what is known and loved. At the same time, I hope that even the most knowledgeable devotees will sometimes feel their memory, or their wits, stretched to the full, as they work their way through the following pages.

M.L.

King Henry V

Across

1 Cry 'God for Harry! ... and Saint George!' (7)
7 I would give all my ... for a pot of ale and safety (4)
8 This day is called the ... of Crispian (5)
9 I think the king is but a man, as I ... (2)
11 He today that sheds his blood with me shall be my ... (7)
12 Can this cockpit hold the ... fields of France? (5)
13 We happy ..., we band of brothers (3)
14 Good yeomen, whose ... were made in England (5)
17 Then will he strip his .. and show his scars (6)
19 From Ireland coming, bringing ... (9)
22 Then ... we in, to know his embassy (2)
23 He that shall live this ... and see old age (3)
24 Or close the ... up with our English dead! (4)

King Henry V

Down

2 Not for Cadwallader and all his … (5)
3 Teach the … of order to a peopled kingdom (3)
4 Once more unto the breach, … friends (4)
5 Trust none, for … are straws (5)
6 Then lend the eye a … aspect (8)
10 I pray thee wish not one man … (4)
12 There is much care and … in this Welshman (6)
13 It is not the … for maids in France to kiss before they are married (7)
15 O God of battles! steel … soldiers' hearts (2)
16 The violet … to him as it doth to me (6)
18 Will yearly on the … feast his neighbours (5)
20 Compound a …, half-French, half-English (3)
21 And gentlemen of England … abed (3)

Flowers and Herbs

1. To gild refined gold, to paint the …
2. There's …, that's for remembrance
3. The azured …, like thy veins
4. I know a bank whereon the wild … blows
5. The …, that goes to bed with the sun, and with him rises weeping
6. That which we call a …, by any other name would smell as sweet
7. Here, in this place, I'll set a bank of …, sour herb of grace
8. Himself the … path of dalliance treads
9. A … in the youth of primy nature
10. Here's flowers for you; hot lavender, mints, savory, …
11. When … pied and violets blue and lady-smocks all silver-white
12. Not …, nor mandragora, nor all the drowsy syrups of the world

    Daisies   Harebell   Lily   Marigold   Marjoram   Poppy   Primrose   Rose   Rosemary

    Rue   Thyme   Violet

Two Gentlemen of Verona

Heroines

```
A I T R O P E R D I T A
I L M I C H A O E A A R
L B O P H E L I A C L T
E E J I T I R N I N A A
C A O A V H O S N A N P
R T K I B M S A T I A O
E R A T E E A E N B I E
S I W D J U L I E T R L
S C S U E S I L V I A C
I E L S T C N E G O M I
D I O O M A D N A R I M
A N E L E H E R M I A B
```

Beatrice	Juliet
Bianca	Kate
Celia	Miranda
Cleopatra	Mariana
Cressida	Olivia
Desdemona	Ophelia
Helena	Perdita
Hermia	Portia
Imogen	Rosalind
Jessica	Silvia
Julia	Viola

Royal Personages

Fill in the first names

1. ..., Queen of Denmark
2. ..., King of Naples
3. ..., Count of Rousillon
4. ..., Prince of Bohemia
5. ..., Queen of the Amazons
6. ..., Duke of Milan
7. ..., King of Sicilia
8. ..., Prince of Tyre
9. ..., King of Troy
10. ..., Queen of the Goths
11. ..., Prince of Arragon
12. ..., Duke of Illyria

Othello

Across

2 Though in the trade of ... I have slain men (3)
7 ... catch my soul but I do love thee (9)
8 An old black ... is tupping your white ewe (3)
9 I will play the swan, and die ... music (2)
10 All masters cannot ... truly followed (2)
13 Of the Cannibals that each other ... (3)
14 The ... bosom of such a thing as you (5)
15 Who steals my purse steals ... (5)
19 Whip me, ... devils, from the possession of this heavenly sight (2)
20 My parts, my ..., and my perfect soul (5)
21 The more ... she, and you the blacker devil (5)
22 Make the Moor thank ... (2)
23 To ... fools and chronicle small beer (6)

Othello

Down

1. Be thus when thou ... dead, and I will kill thee (3)
2. Of one that loved not ... but too well (6)
3. Had tongue ... will and yet was never loud (2)
4. Threw a pearl away ... than all his tribe (6)
5. Her head ... her knee, sing willow (2)
6. O! beware, my lord, of ... (8)
7. She gave me for my ... a world of sighs (5)
11. Some ... villain, some busy and insinuating rogue (7)
12. It is the green-eyed ... which doth mock (7)
16. If ... would make me such another world (6)
17. Her salt ... fell from her, and softened the stones (5)
18. There's ... in the web of it (5)
20. I will a round unvarnished ... deliver (4)

Birds

1. The … is hoarse that croaks the fatal entrance of Duncan
2. In a cowslip's bell I lie, there I couch when … do cry
3. … have built in Cleopatra's sails their nests
4. The thrush and the … are summer songs for me and my aunt
5. Light thickens, and the … makes wing to the rooky wood
6. A lover's eye will gaze an … blind
7. The … at heaven's gate sings
8. I will wear my heart on my sleeve for … to peck at
9. The poor …, the most diminutive of birds
10. So doth the … her downy cygnets save
11. There's a special providence in the fall of a …
12. My …, we have beat them to their beds

    Crow   Daws   Eagle   Jay   Lark   Nightingale   Owls   Raven   Sparrow

    Swallows   Swan   Wren

Twelfth Night

Heroes

```
F E C S U M U H T S O P
L E V A L E N T I N E O
O O R M B E R T R A M B
R A G D E E O R S I N O
I O S U I L U J B T B O
Z L M A N N N E E S A L
E S T E L M A H N A S L
L T O K O N E N E B S E
S U I R T E M E D E A H
B P R O T E U S I S N T
I S N P E T R U C H I O
L Y S A N D E R K H O O
```

Antony	Lysander
Bassanio	Orsino
Benedick	Othello
Bertram	Petruchio
Demetrius	Posthumus
Edgar	Proteus
Ferdinand	Romeo
Florizel	Sebastian
Hamlet	Valentine
Julius	

Occupations

What was the occupation of

1. Quince
2. Bottom
3. Starveling
4. Christopher Sly
5. Holofernes
6. Elbow
7. Angelo
8. Francisca
9. Cinna
10. Sir Hugh Evans
11. Abhorson
12. Mopsa and Dorcas

Macbeth

Across

1. 'Fear not, till Birnam wood … come to Dunsinane' (2)
2. The … way to the everlasting bonfire (8)
6. Bring forth … children only (3)
7. Out, damned …! out, I say (4)
9. All my pretty chickens and their … (3)
10. Nothing in his life became him like the leaving … (2)
11. I may tell pale-hearted … it lies (4)
12. Screw your courage to the … place (8)
14. There's daggers in men's … (6)
16. Upon this blasted … you stop our way (5)
18. There's no art to … the mind's construction in the face (4)
20. Good things of day begin … droop and drowse (2)
21. If chance will have … king (2)
22. To the last … of recorded time (8)

Macbeth

Down

1 The attempt and not the ... confounds us (4)
3 Like valour's ... carved out his passage (6)
4 I have ... full with horrors (6)
5 Vaulting ..., which o'erleaps itself (8)
6 Too full of the ... of human kindness (4)
8 These ... dreams that shake us nightly (8)
13 Will all ... Neptune's ocean wash this blood clean from my hand? (5)
15 But here, upon this bank and ... of time (5)
17 Double, double ... and trouble (4)
18 ...! a soldier, and afeard? (3)
19 Time and the hour runs through the roughest ... (3)
21 'Amen' stuck in ... throat (2)

Colours

1. My salad days, when I was … in judgement
2. Like the … drops in the bottom of a cowslip
3. The poop was burnished gold, … the sails
4. Pluck a … rose from off this thorn with me
5. A forked mountain, or … promontory, with trees upon it
6. This precious stone, set in a … sea
7. Dapples the drowsy east with spots of …
8. Plumpy Bacchus, with … eyne
9. But look, the morn, in … mantle clad
10. Henceforth, the … hand of a lady fever thee
11. And cuckoo-buds of … hue do paint the meadows with delight
12. … lads and girls all must, like chimney sweepers, come to dust

Blue   Crimson   Golden   Green   Grey   Pink   Purple   Red   Russet   Silver   White   Yellow

As You Like It

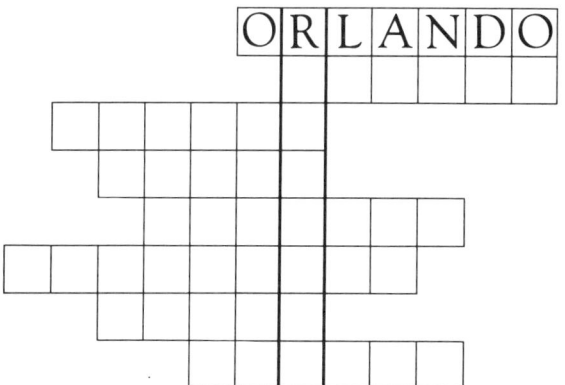

Place Names

```
P B W R E S U C A R Y S
A D A I S T S U R P Y C
I O U S N A L I M O N N
R V D N O D L H R E A O
D E A E S A S T R V C L
N R P H S I M O A E S L
A O R T F A N R R N U I
X N O A N I R A R I T S
E A D T S E R D N C C U
L L U L M D O S I E E O
A A E O E D I N G S L R
E M R N A N I S S E M I
```

Alexandria	Padua
Arden	Rome
Athens	Rousillon
Cyprus	Sardis
Dover	Syracuse
Dunsinane	Troy
Elsinore	Tuscany
Mantua	Venice
Messina	Verona
Milan	Windsor
Navarre	

Waiting Women

Whom did they serve

1. Lucetta
2. Margaret and Ursula
3. Rosaline, Maria and Katherine
4. Nerissa
5. Maria
6. Emilia
7. Alice
8. Patience and Anne Bullen
9. Nurse
10. Charmian and Iras
11. Helen
12. Lychorida

Hamlet

Across

1 With mirth in funeral and with … in marriage (5)
6 There was … such stuff in my thoughts (2)
7 I am native here, and to the manner … (4)
8 To thine own self be … (4)
9 I shall not look upon his like … (5)
10 To sleep, perchance to … (5)
12 A little more than …, and less than kind (3)
14 The bird of dawning singeth all night … (4)
15 … thee to a nunnery (3)
16 What's Hecuba to him, or … to Hecuba? (2)
17 There are more things in heaven and earth, … (7)
20 O! that this too … solid flesh would melt (3)
21 Though … be madness, yet there be method in it (4)
22 Brevity is the … of wit (4)
23 Lord Hamlet is a prince, out of thy … (4)

Hamlet

Down

1 Something is rotten in the state of ... (7)
2 Be thou a spirit of health or ... damned (6)
3 Neither a borrower nor a ... be (6)
4 The thousand ... shocks that flesh is heir to (7)
5 I must be ..., only to be kind (5)
10 Conscience ... make cowards of us all (4)
11 When we have shuffled off this ... coil (6)
13 Be thou as chaste as ..., as pure as snow (3)
15 It is an honest ..., that let me tell you (5)
16 No ... upon his head, his stockings fouled (3)
18 This majestical ... fretted with golden fire (4)
19 For the apparel ... proclaims the man (3)
20 That he is mad, ... true (3)

Animals

1. Sweet words, low-crooked curtsies, and base … fawning
2. We were as twinned … that did frisk in the sun
3. Against the Capitol I met a … who glared upon me
4. Treason is but trusted like the …
5. O, for a … with wings
6. I see you strain like … in the slips
7. I had rather be a … and live upon the vapour of a dungeon
8. They will eat like … and fight like devils
9. In time the savage … doth bear the yoke
10. She will sing the savageness out of a …
11. Eye of newt and toe of frog, wool of … and tongue of dog
12. Why should a dog, a horse, a … have life, and thou no breath at all?

Bat   Bear   Bull   Fox   Greyhounds   Horse   Lambs   Lion   Rat

Spaniel   Toad   Wolves

The Winter's Tale

Fools and Fairies

```
M O S S O L B E S A E P
P E B I B S P E E D L U
E N U L E I R A U E E C
L O L A R O V L O E M K
B T L I O I L L K S E B
O S C N N T U F E D D E
W H A A Y C R R R R F W
O C L T N D E A A A E B
D U F I E C L T W T E O
A O R T D B S U E S B C
H T J U N O N N O U L I
S I R I C E H T O M E Z
```

- Ariel
- Bullcalf
- Ceres
- Cobweb
- Costard
- Dull
- Elbow
- Feeble
- Iris
- Juno
- Moth
- Mouldy
- Mustardseed
- Oberon
- Peaseblossom
- Puck
- Shadow
- Speed
- Titania
- Touchstone
- Trinculo

Fathers and Daughters

Name the father of

1. Juliet
2. Hermia
3. Jessica
4. Celia
5. Bianca
6. Blanch
7. Cassandra
8. Lavinia
9. Ophelia
10. Goneril
11. Imogen
12. Desdemona

King Lear

Across

1. How sharper than a serpent's tooth it is to have a … child! (9)
5. … not his ghost: O! let him pass (3)
6. As flies to … boys are we to the gods (6)
9. These late … in the sun and moon portend no good to us (8)
10. Striving to better, … we mar what's well (3)
11. A poor old man, as full of grief as … (3)
15. Nature in you stands … the very verge of her confine (2)
16. Out, … jelly! (4)
17. I have no way, and therefore want no … (4)
19. Men must endure their going hence, even as their coming … (6)
22. You cataracts and hurricanes, … (5)
23. You have that in your countenance which I would fain call … (6)

King Lear

Down

1. Child Roland to the dark ... came (5)
2. Speak less than thou ... (7)
3. I am a man more sinned against than ... (7)
4. Take physic, pomp; ... thyself to feel what wretches feel (6)
7. She .. herself a dowry (2)
8. We two ... will sing like birds in the cage (5)
11. Give me ... ounce of civet, good apothecary (2)
12. Her voice was ... soft, gentle and low (4)
13. The gods are just, and of our pleasant vices make instruments to ... us (6)
14. Winter's not gone yet, if the wild ... fly that way (5)
15. Who loses and who wins; who's in, who's ... (3)
18. That way madness lies; let me ... that (4)
20. If ... be true, all vengeance comes too short (2)
21. Upon the rack of this tough world stretch .. out longer (3)

Apparel

1. That … did an Egyptian to my mother give
2. Leathern wings to make my small elves …
3. He will come in yellow …, and 'tis a colour she abhors
4. A brushes his … a mornings, what should that bode
5. For he was more than over … in love
6. His youthful … well saved a world too wide for his shrunk shank
7. They threw their … as they would hang them on the horns of the moon
8. A man may wear it on both sides, as a leather …
9. You all do know this …; I remember the first time Caesar ever put it on
10. He bought his doublet in Italy, his round hose in France, his … in Germany
11. O! that I were a … upon that hand, that I might touch that cheek
12. King Stephen was a worthy peer, his … cost him but a crown

Bonnet Breeches Caps Coats Glove Handkerchief Hat Hose Jerkin Mantle Shoes Stockings

Much Ado About Nothing

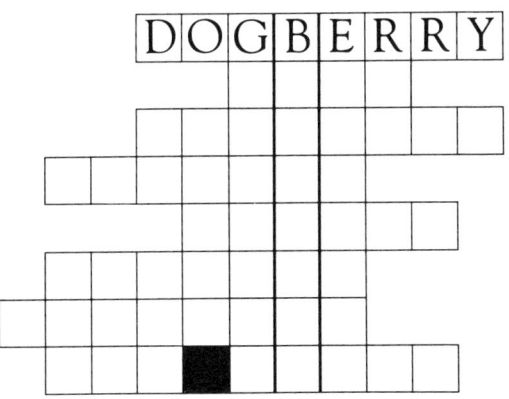

My Lords

Which British place names completes the following titles

1. Richard Plantagenet, Duke of
2. Henry Percy, Earl of
3. Geffrey Fitzpeter, Earl of
4. Thomas Mowbray, Duke of
5. John Morton, Bishop of
6. Edmund Mortimer, Earl of
7. William Mareshall, Earl of
8. Thomas Beaufort, Duke of
9. Henry Beaufort, Bishop of
10. Henry Bolingbroke, Duke of
11. William Longsword, Earl of
12. John of Gaunt, Duke of

Masters and Men

Whom did they serve

1. Robin
2. Abram
3. Simple
4. Dromio
5. Pindarus
6. Philemon
7. Rugby
8. Moth
9. Leonardo
10. Davy
11. Adam and Dennis
12. Grumio and Curtis

Julius Caesar

Across

1 Not that I loved … less, but that I loved Rome more (6)
6 I am no …, as Brutus is (6)
7 There is a … in the affairs of men (4)
11 He doth … the narrow world, like a Colossus (8)
14 … a huge mountain 'tween my heart and tongue (3)
15 For I have neither …, nor words, nor worth (3)
16 As I live to … in awe of such a thing as I myself (2)
17 I had rather be a …, and bay the moon (3)
19 O mighty Caesar! dost thou lie so …? (3)
23 … very like: he hath the falling sickness (3)
25 He loves … plays, as thou dost, Antony (2)
26 … should be made of sterner stuff (8)
28 This was the noblest Roman of them … (3)
30 If you have …, prepare to shed them now (5)
31 Yond … has a lean and hungry look (7)
32 For who … firm that cannot be seduced? (2)

Julius Caesar

Down

1. This was the most unkindest ... of all (3)
2. But it sufficeth that the day will ... (3)
3. They ... the Hybla bees, and leave them honeyless (3)
4. The valiant never ... of death but once (5)
5. How hard it is for women to keep ... (7)
8. Beware the ... of March (4)
9. Let me have men about me that are ... (3)
10. It is the ... day that brings forth the adder (5)
12. We are ... lions littered in one day (3)
13. For mine own part, ... was Greek to me (2)
17. Ambition's ... is paid (4)
18. You blocks, you ..., you worse than senseless things (6)
20. My credit now stands ... such slippery ground (2)
21. Get the start of the majestic ... and bear the palm alone (5)
22. Cry '...' and let slip the dogs of war (5)
24. The fault, dear Brutus, is not ... our stars (2)
27. He is a dreamer; let us leave him: ... (4)
29. Let's carve him ... a dish fit for gods (2)
30. Et ... Brute! (2)

Food and Drink

1. I had rather live with ... and garlic in a windmill
2. The justice in fair round belly with ... lined
3. I love long life better than ...
4. Give them great meals of ... and iron and steel
5. His brain which is as dry as the remainder ... after a voyage
6. What say you to a piece of beef and ...?
7. There shall be in England seven halfpenny ... sold for a penny
8. If sack and ... be a fault, God help the wicked
9. The funeral baked ... did coldly furnish forth the marriage tables
10. For a quart of ... is a dish for a king
11. And ... comes frozen home in pail
12. Dost thou think, because thou art virtuous, there shall be no more ... and ale?

   Ale   Beef   Biscuit   Cakes   Capon   Cheese   Figs   Loaves   Meats

   Milk   Mustard   Sugar

Measure for Measure

Answers

Page

5 **KING HENRY V (across)** 1 England. 7 Fame. 8 Feast. 9 Am. 11 Brother. 12 Vasty. 13 Few. 14 Limbs. 17 Sleeve. 19 Rebellion. 22 Go. 23 Day. 24 Wall. **(down)** 2 Goats. 3 Act. 4 Dear. 5 Oaths. 6 Terrible. 10 More. 12 Valour. 13 Fashion. 15 My. 16 Smells. 18 Vigil. 20 Boy. 21 Now.

6 **FLOWERS AND HERBS** 1 Lily. 2 Rosemary. 3 Harebell. 4 Thyme. 5 Marigold. 6 Rose. 7 Rue. 8 Primrose. 9 Violet. 10 Marjoram. 11 Daisies. 12 Poppy.

7 **TWO GENTLEMEN OF VERONA** Speed, Silvia, Launce, Proteus, Thurio, Julia, Valentine, Eglamour. **(down)** Panthino.

9 **ROYAL PERSONAGES** 1 Gertrude. 2 Alonso. 3 Bertram. 4 Florizel. 5 Hippolyta. 6 Prospero. 7 Leontes. 8 Pericles. 9 Priam. 10 Tamora. 11 Don Pedro. 12 Orsino.

11 **OTHELLO (across)** 2 War. 7 Perdition. 8 Ram. 9 In. 10 Be. 13 Eat. 14 Sooty. 15 Trash. 19 Ye. 20 Title. 21 Angel. 22 Me. 23 Suckle. **(down)** 1 Art. 2 Wisely. 3 At. 4 Richer. 5 On. 6 Jealousy. 7 Pains. 11 Eternal. 12 Monster. 16 Heaven. 17 Tears. 18 Magic. 20 Tale.

12 **BIRDS** 1 Raven. 2 Owls. 3 Swallows. 4 Jay. 5 Crow. 6 Eagle. 7 Lark. 8 Daws. 9 Wren. 10 Swan. 11 Sparrow. 12 Nightingale.

Page

13 **TWELFTH NIGHT** Maria, Sebastian, Valentine, Olivia, Orsino, Viola, Antonio, Sir Toby Belch. **(down)** Malvolio.

15 **OCCUPATIONS** 1 Carpenter. 2 Weaver. 3 Tailor. 4 Tinker. 5 Schoolmaster. 6 Constable. 7 Goldsmith. 8 Nun. 9 Poet. 10 Parson. 11 Executioner. 12 Shepherdesses.

17 **MACBETH (across)** 1 Do. 2 Primrose. 6 Men. 7 Spot. 9 Dam. 10 It. 11 Fear. 12 Sticking. 14 Smiles. 16 Heath. 18 Find. 20 To. 21 Me. 22 Syllable. **(down)** 1 Deed. 3 Minion. 4 Supped. 5 Ambition. 6 Milk. 8 Terrible. 13 Great. 15 Shoal. 17 Toil. 18 Fie. 19 Day. 21 My.

18 **COLOURS** 1 Green. 2 Crimson. 3 Purple. 4 Red. 5 Blue. 6 Silver. 7 Grey. 8 Pink. 9 Russet. 10 White. 11 Yellow. 12 Golden.

19 **AS YOU LIKE IT** Orlando, Oliver, Jaques, Celia, William, Frederick, Corin, Audrey. **(down)** Rosalind.

21 **WAITING WOMEN** 1 Julia. 2 Hero. 3 Princess of France. 4 Portia. 5 Olivia. 6 Hermione. 7 Katherine, Princess of France. 8 Queen Katherine. 9 Juliet. 10 Cleopatra. 11 Imogen. 12 Marina.

Answers

Page

23 **HAMLET (across)** 1 Dirge. 6 No. 7 Born. 8 True. 9 Again. 10 Dream. 12 Kin. 14 Long. 15 Get. 16 He. 17 Horatio. 20 Too. 21 This. 22 Soul. 23 Star. **(down)** 1 Denmark. 2 Goblin. 3 Lender. 4 Natural. 5 Cruel. 10 Doth. 11 Mortal. 13 Ice. 15 Ghost. 16 Hat. 18 Roof. 19 Oft. 20 Tis.

24 **ANIMALS** 1 Spaniel. 2 Lambs. 3 Lion. 4 Fox. 5 Horse. 6 Greyhounds. 7 Toad. 8 Wolves. 9 Bull. 10 Bear. 11 Bat. 12 Rat.

25 **THE WINTER'S TALE** Mopsa, Hermione, Florizel, Dorcas, Mamillius, Leontes, Camillo. **(down)** Perdita.

27 **FATHERS AND DAUGHTERS** 1 Capulet. 2 Egeus. 3 Shylock. 4 Frederick. 5 Baptista. 6 Alphonso. 7 Priam. 8 Titus Andronicus. 9 Polonius. 10. Lear. 11 Cymbeline. 12 Brabantio.

29 **KING LEAR (across)** 1 Thankless. 5 Vex. 6 Wanton. 9 Eclipses. 10 Oft. 11 Age. 15 On. 16 Vile. 17 Eyes. 19 Hither. 22 Spout. 23 Master. **(down)** 1 Tower. 2 Knowest. 3 Sinning. 4 Expose. 7 Is. 8 Alone. 11 An. 12 Ever. 13 Plague. 14 Geese. 15 Out. 18 Shun. 20 It. 21 Him.

30 **APPAREL** 1 Handkerchief. 2 Coats. 3 Stockings. 4 Hat. 5 Shoes. 6 Hose. 7 Caps. 8 Jerkin. 9 Mantle. 10 Bonnet. 11 Glove. 12 Breeches.

Page

31 **MUCH ADO ABOUT NOTHING** Dogberry, Hero, Borachio, Leonato, Verges, Claudio, Benedick, Don Pedro. **(down)** Beatrice.

32 **MY LORDS** 1. York. 2 Northumberland. 3 Essex. 4 Norfolk. 5 Ely. 6 March. 7 Pembroke. 8 Exeter. 9 Winchester. 10 Hereford. 11 Salisbury. 12 Lancaster.

33 **MASTERS AND MEN** 1 Falstaff. 2 Montague. 3 Slender. 4 Antipholus. 5 Cassius. 6 Cerimon. 7 Doctor Caius. 8 Armado. 9 Bassanio. 10 Shallow. 11 Oliver. 12 Petruchio.

35 **JULIUS CAESAR (across)** 1 Caesar. 6 Orator. 7 Tide. 11 Bestride. 14 Set. 15 Wit. 16 Be. 17 Dog. 19 Low. 23 Tis. 25 No. 26 Ambition. 28 All. 30 Tears. 31 Cassius. 32 So. **(down)** 1 Cut. 2 End. 3 Rob. 4 Taste. 5 Counsel. 8 Ides. 9 Fat. 10 Bright. 12 Two. 13 It. 17 Debt. 18 Stones. 20 On. 21 World. 22 Havoc. 24 In. 27 Pass. 29 As. 30 Tu.

36 **FOOD AND DRINK** 1 Cheese. 2 Capon. 3 Figs. 4 Beef. 5 Biscuit. 6 Mustard. 7 Loaves. 8 Sugar. 9 Meats. 10 Ale. 11 Milk. 12 Cakes.

37 **MEASURE FOR MEASURE** Froth, Peter, Varrius, Angelo, Escalus, Juliet, Isabella, Lucio, Mariana. **(down)** Francisca.

ABSON BOOKS

Other books in preparation in this Quiz and Puzzle series include:- Charles Dickens, Thomas Hardy, Mrs Gaskell, George Eliot and Sherlock Holmes.

Available now:-
THE JANE AUSTEN QUIZ AND PUZZLE BOOK
by Maggie Lane - £1.75
A variety of puzzles and quizzes designed to test your knowledge of the novels of Jane Austen. All the answers may be found in the six novels and are included in the back of the book.

THE BRONTE SISTERS QUIZ AND PUZZLE BOOK
by Maggie Lane - £1.75
This is based on the seven novels of Charlotte, Emily and Anne with illustrations by Edmund Dulac.

AMERICAN ENGLISH/ENGLISH AMERICAN - 95p
A glossary of everday words which have completely different meanings depending upon which side of the Atlantic you happen to be.

RHYMING COCKNEY SLANG - 95p
A glossary to help you use your loaf (of bread - head) in getting about London.

SCOTTISH ENGLISH/ENGLISH SCOTTISH - 95p
A glossary of everyday Scottish words. Informative for newcomers and visitors - evocative for expatriates.

IRISH ENGLISH/ENGLISH IRISH - 95p
A glossary of words to help disentangle the delightful Irish gift of the gab. This includes a section on the vocabulary associated with the *troubles*.

AUSTRALIAN ENGLISH/ENGLISH AUSTRALIAN - 99p
A glossary of words helpful to all who journey to or from the world's largest island and smallest continent.

MAGENTA/MARATHON/MECCA - 95p
Why is it that *magenta* is a colour, a huge task a *marathon,* and Lords can be termed the *Mecca* of cricket? The origins of these and 200 more fascinating toponyms are listed in this little glossary.

YIDDISH ENGLISH/ENGLISH YIDDISH - 95p
Shlep, shlock, shmaltz, are included in this glossary of words which constantly crop up in literature, films, on television and the radio.

A full list of Abson books will be sent on request.

 All available from booksellers or by adding 20p for the first copy and 10p per copy thereafter for packing and postage from the publishers, Abson Books, Abson, Wick, Bristol BS15 5TT.